THE MUSIC KIT
SCOREBOOK

TOM MANOFF W·W· Norton & Company · Inc · New York

SCOREBOOK DESIGNED BY ELSA ANN DANENBERG

Copyright © 1976 by Tom Manoff. All rights reserved.
Published simultaneously in Canada by George J. McLeod Limited, Toronto.
Printed in the United States of America.

First Edition

Library of Congress Cataloging in Publication Data

Manoff, Tom.
  The music kit.
    CONTENTS: [1] Workbook.—[2] Rhythm reader.—
[3] Scorebook.
    1. Music—Theory, Elementary.   I. Title.
    MT7.M267   781   76-1006
    ISBN 0-393-09179-1

1 2 3 4 5 6 7 8 9 0

CONTENTS

1. *The Trees They Do Grow High*   Traditional   1
2. *I Know Where I'm Going*   Traditional   2
3. *Greensleeves*   Traditional   3
4. *One Grain of Sand*   Appalachian Lullaby   4
5. *The Water Is Wide*   Traditional   5
6. *The Riddle Song*   Traditional   6
7. *Drink to Me Only with Thine Eyes*   Traditional English   7
8. *Lullaby*   Johannes Brahms   8
9. *Barbrie Allen*   Traditional English   9
10. *Believe Me, If All Those Endearing Young Charms*   Traditional   10
11. *Shoo Fly*   Traditional American   11
12. *Down in the Valley*   Traditional American   12
13. *Dona, Dona*   Traditional Hebrew   13
14. *Black, Black, Black*   Traditional American   15
15. *Wayfaring Stranger*   Traditional American   16
16. *The Wraggle-Taggle Gypsies, O!*   Traditional English   17
17. *Hush, Little Baby*   Traditional   18
18. *This Old Man*   Traditional Game Song   19
19. *Johnny Has Gone for a Soldier*   Traditional American   20
20. *Alouette*   French-Canadian Game Song   21
21. *Go Down, Moses*   Spiritual   22
22. *The Cowboy's Lament*   Traditional American   23
23. *Cherry Blooms*   Traditional Japanese   24
24. *All Beauty Within You*   Traditional Italian   25
25. *Dance of Zalongo*   Traditional Greek   26
26. *Jeune Fillette*   Traditional French   27
27. *Philis, Plus Avare que Tendre*   Traditional French   28
28. *Que ne suis-je la Fougère*   Traditional French   29
29. *Melody*   Traditional Finnish   30
30. *Ho There, Brother*   Traditional Yugoslavian   31
31. *Silent Night*   Franz Gruber   32
32. *The First Noel*   Traditional Carol   33
33. *America the Beautiful*   Samuel A. Ward   34
34. *America*   Henry Carey (?)   36
35. *Oh, How Lovely Is the Evening*   German Round   37
36. *Hey, Ho, Nobody at Home*   English Round   38
37. *Dona Nobis Pacem*   Traditional Round   39
38. *Shalom Chaverim*   Israeli Round   40
39. *The Welcome Song*   18th-Century American Canon   41
40. *Victimae Paschali*   Wipo   42
41. *Adieu, Sweet Amarillis*   John Wilbye   43
42. *The Young Convert*   19th-Century New England Hymn   49
43. *Willie, Take Your Little Drum*   Burgundian Carol   51
44. *Remember, O Thou Man*   Thomas Ravenscroft   52
45. *Sarabanda*   Arcangelo Corelli   54
46. *Minuet for Lute*   Robert Visée   55
47. *Minuet*   Henry Purcell   56
48. *Minute, K. 2*   Wolfgang Amadeus Mozart   57
49. *Study in C*   Fernando Sor   59
50. *Ode to Joy*   Ludwig van Beethoven   60
51. *Fugue in C Minor*   Johann Sebastian Bach   61
52. *Waltz in C-Sharp Minor*   Frédéric François Chopin   64
53. *How Strange*   Tom Manoff and Frank Feliciano   73

1 THE TREES THEY DO GROW HIGH

Traditional

1. The trees they do grow high and the leaves they do grow green.
Many is the time my true love I have seen, Many is the hour I've watched him all alone. He's young but he's daily a-growing.

2. Father, dear Father, you've done me great wrong,
   You've married me to a boy who is too young.
   I am twice twelve and he is but fourteen,
   He's young, but he's daily a-growing.

3. Daughter, dear daughter, I've done you no wrong,
   I've married you to a great lord's son.
   He will make a lord for you to wait upon,
   He's young, but he's daily a-growing.

4. At the age of fourteen, he was a married man,
   At the age of fifteen, the father of a son,
   At the age of sixteen, his grave it did grow green,
   And death put an end to his growing.

2 I KNOW WHERE I'M GOING

Traditional

1. I know where I'm going, and I know who's going with me; I know who I love, but the dear knows who I'll marry.
2. Feather beds are soft, and painted rooms are bonnie; But I would trade them all for my handsome, winsome Johnnie.
3. I have stockings of silk, and shoes of bright green leather; Combs to buckle my hair, and a ring for every finger.
4. Some say he's bad, but I say he's bonnie; Fairest of them all is my handsome, winsome Johnnie.

③ GREENSLEEVES

Traditional

4 ONE GRAIN OF SAND

Appalachian Lullaby

Rhythm freely improvised

1. One grain of sand,____ one grain of sand ____ in all the world;

One grain of sand,____ one lit-tle boy, one lit-tle girl.

2. One drop of rain, one drop of rain on all the land;
   One drop of rain, one little hand in all my hand.

3. One little star, one little star up in the blue;
   One little star, one little me, one little you.

4. One grain of sand, one grain of sand in all the world;
   One grain of sand, one little boy, one little girl.

5 THE WATER IS WIDE

6 THE RIDDLE SONG

Traditional

1. I gave my love a cher-ry that has no stone. I gave my love a chick-en that has no bone. I gave my love a sto-ry that has no end. I_____ gave my love a ba-by with no cry-ing!

3. A cherry when its blooming, it has no stone.
   A chicken when its pipping, it has no bone.
   The story of "I love you," it has no end.
   A baby when its sleeping, there's no crying.

2. How can there be a cherry that has no stone?
   How can there be a chicken that has no bone?
   How can there be a story that has no end?
   How can there be a baby with no crying?

7 DRINK TO ME ONLY WITH THINE EYES

Words by Ben Jonson (1616)
Traditional English

Drink to me only with thine eyes, And I will pledge with mine;
Or leave a kiss but in the cup, And I'll not ask for wine. The
thirst that from the soul doth rise, Doth ask a drink divine:
But might I of Jove's nectar sup, I would not change for thine.

2. I sent thee late a rosy wreath,
   Not so much honoring thee,
   As giving it a hope, that there
   It could not withered be.

   But thou thereon did'st only breathe,
   And sent'st it back to me;
   Since when it grows and smells, I swear,
   Not of itself, but thee.

⑧ LULLABY

Johannes Brahms
1833–1897

9 BARBRIE ALLEN

Traditional English

1. In Scarlet-town where I was born, There was a fair maid dwelling, Made ev-'ry youth cry "Well a-day," Her name was Barbrie Allen.

2. All in the merry month of May,
   When green buds they were swelling,
   Young Jonny Grove on his deathbed lay,
   For love of Barbrie Allen.

3. He sent his man unto her then
   To the town where she was dwelling:
   "You must come to my master, dear,
   If your name be Barbrie Allen."

4. So slowly, slowly she came up,
   And slowly she came nigh him,
   And all she said when there she came:
   "Young man, I think you're dying!"

5. He turned his face unto the wall,
   And death was drawing nigh him:
   "Adieu, adieu, my dear friends all,
   Be kind to Barbrie Allen."

10 BELIEVE ME, IF ALL THOSE ENDEARING YOUNG CHARMS

Words by Thomas Moore (1808) **Traditional**

11 SHOO FLY

Traditional American

Shoo fly, don't both-er me, Shoo fly, don't both-er me,

Shoo fly, don't both-er me, For I be-long to some-bod-y.

I feel, I feel, I feel like a morn-ing star, I feel, I feel, I

feel like a morn-ing star.

(Da Capo al Fine)

2. I feel, I feel, that's what my Mother said,
   Like angels pouring molasses upon my head.

12 DOWN IN THE VALLEY

Traditional American

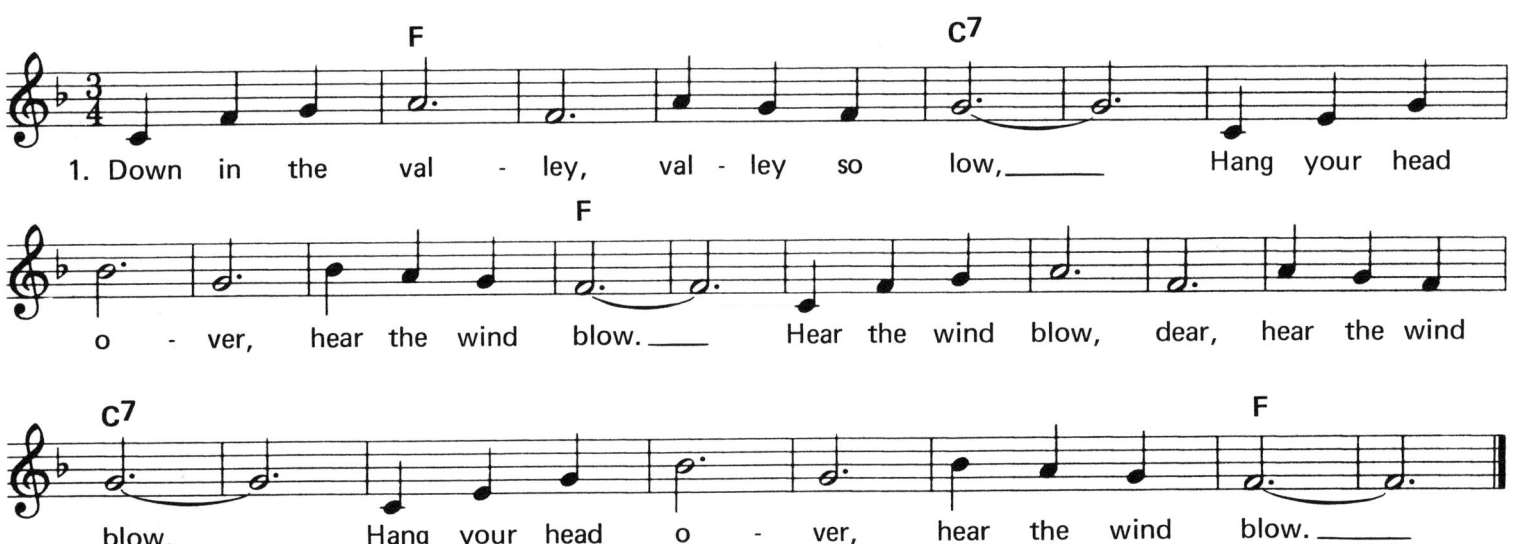

2. Writing this letter, containing three lines,
   Answer my question, will you be mine?
   Will you be mine, dear, will you be mine?
   Answer my question, will you be mine?

3. Roses love sunshine, violets love dew,
   Angels in heaven know I love you.
   Know I love you, dear, know I love you,
   Angels in heaven know I love you.

Dona, Dona

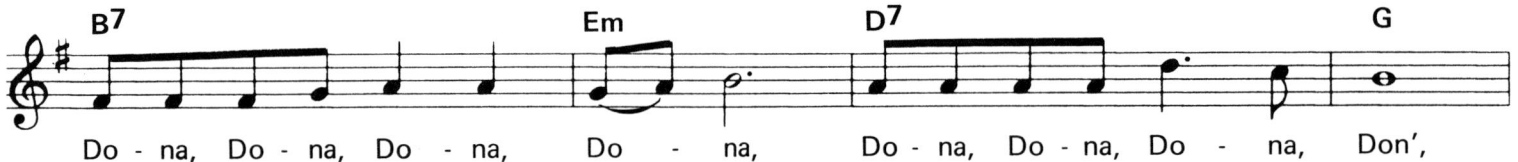

14 BLACK, BLACK, BLACK

Traditional American

1. Black, black, black is the col-or of my true love's hair; Her lips are some-thing won-drous fair; The cool-est brow and the dain-ti-est hands; I love the grass where-on she stands.

2. I love my love and well she knows,
   I love the ground whereon she goes.
   If she no more on earth I'd see,
   My life would quickly leave me.

15 WAYFARING STRANGER

Traditional American

I'm just a poor wayfaring stranger, A-trav'ling through this world of woe, And there's no sickness, toil, or danger In that bright land to which I go. I'm going there to meet my mother, I'm going there no more to roam. I'm just a-going over Jordan, I'm just a-going over home.

16 THE WRAGGLE-TAGGLE GYPSIES, O!

Traditional English

1. There were three gyp-sies a-come to my door, And down-stairs ran this a-la-dy, O! One sang high and the oth-er sang low, And the oth-er sang bon-ny, bon-ny Bis-cay, O!

2. Then she pulled off her silk-finished gown,
   And put on hose of leather, O!
   The ragged, ragged rags about our door,
   And she's gone with the wraggle-taggle Gypsies, O!

3. It was late last night when my lord came home,
   Inquiring for his lady, O!
   The servants cried on every hand,
   She's gone with the wraggle-taggle Gypsies, O!

4. O, saddle to me my milk-white steed,
   And go and fetch me my pony, O!
   That I may ride to seek my bride,
   Who is gone with the wraggle-taggle Gypsies, O!

5. O, he rode high, and he rode low,
   He rode through wood and copses, too,
   Until he came to a wide open field,
   And there he espied his a-lady, O!

6. "What makes you leave your house and land?
   What makes you leave your money, O!
   What makes you leave your new-wedded lord,
   To follow the wraggle-taggle Gypsies, O!"

7. "What care I for my house and my land?
   What care I for my money, O?
   What care I for my new-wedded lord?
   I'm off with the wraggle-taggle Gypsies, O!"

17 HUSH, LITTLE BABY

Traditional

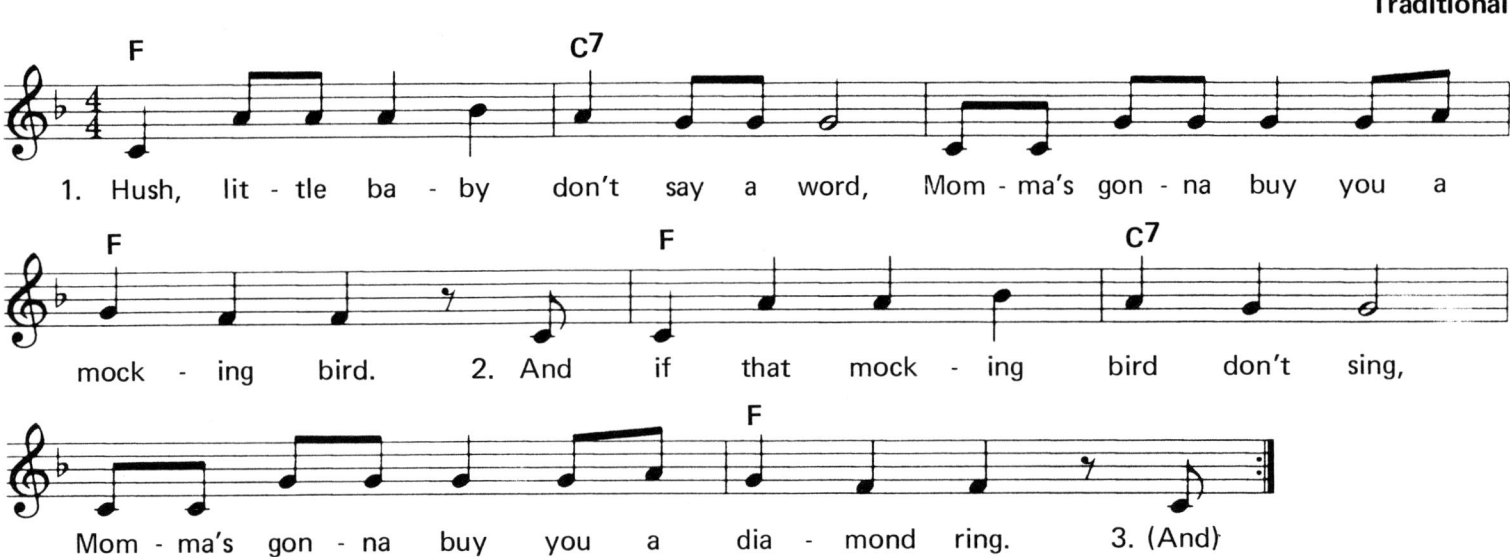

1. Hush, little baby don't say a word, Momma's gonna buy you a mocking bird.
2. And if that mockingbird don't sing, Momma's gonna buy you a diamond ring.

3. If that diamond ring turns brass
   Momma's gonna buy you a looking glass.

4. And if that looking glass gets broke
   Momma's gonna buy you a billy goat.

5. And if that billy goat don't pull
   Momma's gonna buy you a cart and bull.

6. And if that cart and bull turn over
   Momma's gonna buy you a dog named Rover.

7. And if that dog named Rover don't bark
   Momma's gonna buy you a horse and cart.

8. And if that horse and cart fall down
   You'll still be the sweetest little baby in town.

18 THIS OLD MAN

Traditional Game Song

1. This old man, he played one, He played nick nack on his thumb, With a

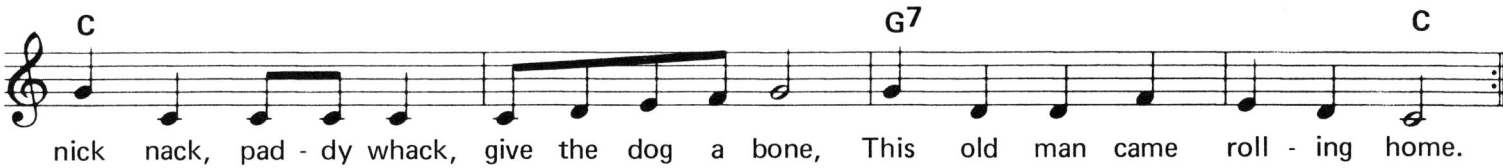

nick nack, pad-dy whack, give the dog a bone, This old man came roll-ing home.

2. This old man, he played two,
   He played nick nack on his shoe,
   With a nick nack, paddy whack, give the dog a bone,
   This old man came rolling home.

3. This old man, he played three,
   He played nick nack on his knee,
   With a nick nack, paddy whack, give the dog a bone,
   This old man came rolling home.

4. This old man, he played four,
   He played nick nack on the door,
   With a nick nack, paddy whack, give the dog a bone,
   This old man came rolling home.

   etc.

19 JOHNNY HAS GONE FOR A SOLDIER

Traditional American

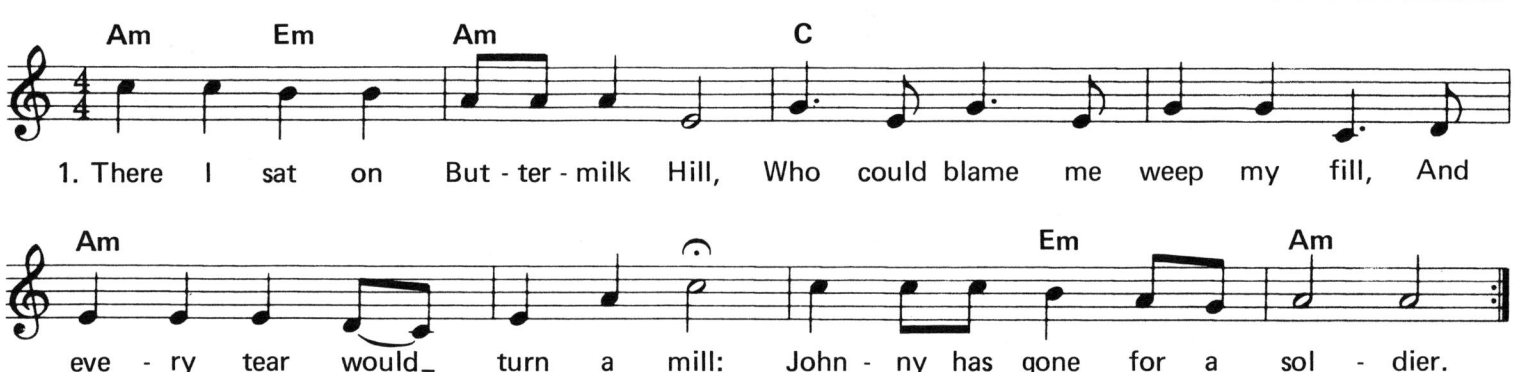

1. There I sat on Buttermilk Hill, Who could blame me weep my fill, And every tear would turn a mill: Johnny has gone for a soldier.

2. Me, oh my, I loved him so,
   Broke my heart to see him go,
   And only time will heal my woe:
   Johnny has gone for a soldier.

20 ALOUETTE

French-Canadian Game Song

Refrain: A-lou-et-te, gen-tille A-lou-et-te, A-lou-et-te, je te plu-me-rai.

Verse: 1. Je te plu-me-rai la tête, je te plu-me-rai la tête. Et la tête, et la tête, A-lou-ette, Oh

2. Je te plumerai le cou, *etc*.

3. Je te plumerai les ailes, *etc*.

4. Je te plumerai les pattes, *etc*.

5. Je te plumerai le dos, *etc*.

6. Je te plumerai la queue, *etc*.

*Repeat all previous verses in reverse order. The last verse will end, "Et la queue, et le dos, et les pattes, et les ailes, et le cou, et la tête."

21 GO DOWN, MOSES

Spiritual

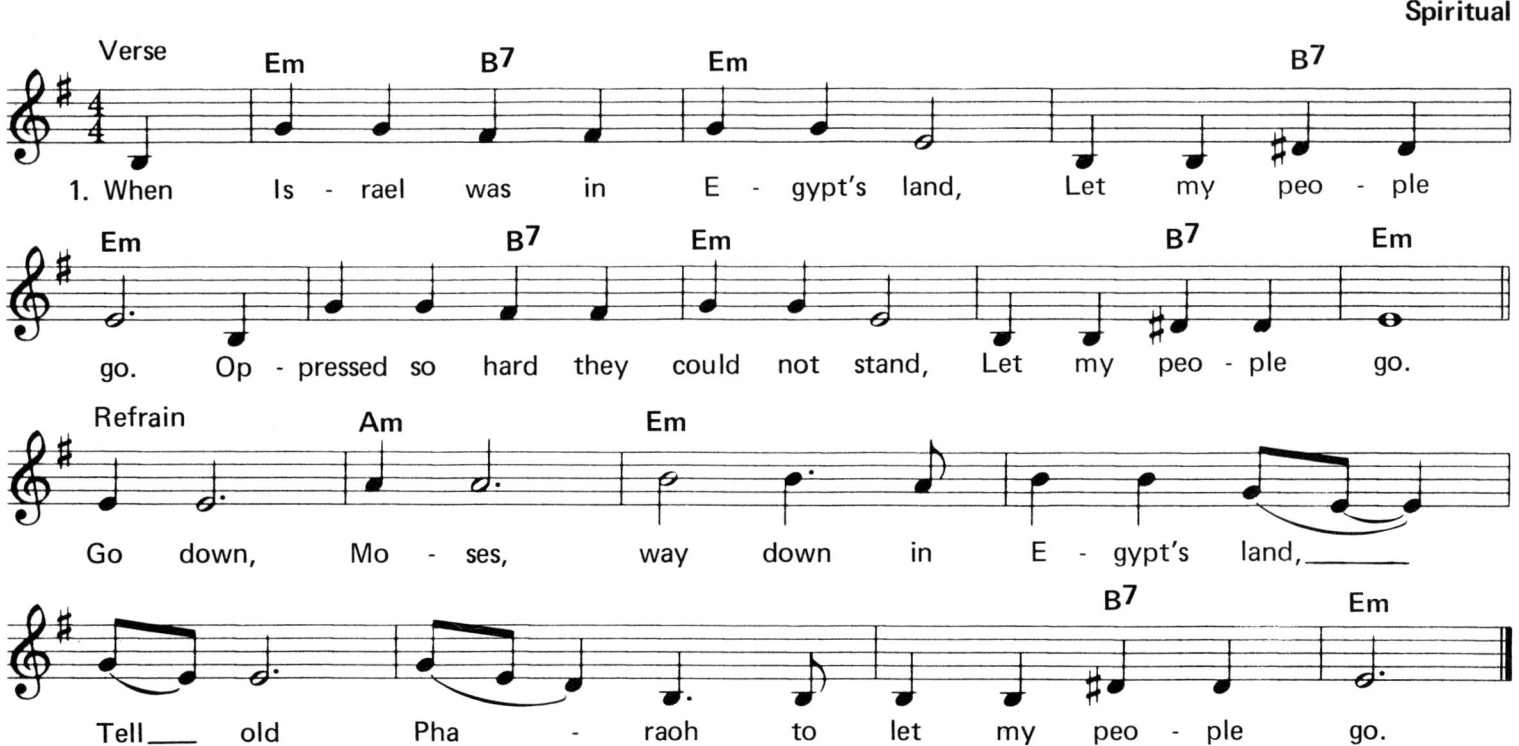

2. Thus spake the Lord, bold Moses said,
 Let my people go.
 If not, I'll smite your first-born dead,

Let my people go.
Go down, Moses, way down in Egypt's land,
Tell old Pharaoh to let my people go.

22 THE COWBOY'S LAMENT

Traditional American

1. As I walked out on the streets of Laredo, As I walked out in Laredo one day, I spied a young cowboy all wrapped in white linen, All wrapped in white linen as cold as the clay.

2. "I see by your outfit that you are a cowboy,"
   These words he did say as I boldly stepped by,
   "Come sit down beside me and hear my sad story,
   I'm shot in the breast and I know I must die."

3. "It was once in the saddle I used to go dashing,
   It was once in the saddle I used to go gay;
   First in the tavern and then in the card house;
   Got shot in the breast and I'm dying today."

4. "Oh beat the drum slowly and play the fife lowly,
   Play the dead march as you bear me along;
   Take me to the valley and lay the sod o'er me,
   For I'm a young cowboy and I know I've done wrong."

23 CHERRY BLOOMS

Traditional Japanese

24 ALL THE BEAUTY WITHIN YOU

Traditional Italian

1. All beauty within you, all graces around you, So late I have found you, so soon we must part! Ah, no, no, no, weep not, take courage, my beauty, To go is my duty, I leave you my heart.

2. I swear to return you the life you have lent me,
   No force shall prevent me, not Death with his dart.
   Ah no, no, no, weep not, take courage, my beauty,
   To go is my duty, I leave you my heart.

25 DANCE OF ZALONGO

Traditional Greek

(Count) 1 2 3 1 2 1 2 1 2 3 1 2 1 2 etc.

26 JEUNE FILLETTE

Traditional French

27 PHILIS, PLUS AVARE QUE TENDRE

Traditional French

28 QUE NE SUIS-JE LA FOUGÈRE

Traditional French

29 MELODY

Traditional Finnish

30 HO THERE, BROTHER

Traditional Yugoslavian

31 SILENT NIGHT

Words by Joseph Mohn
Franz Gruber

32 THE FIRST NOEL

Traditional Carol

America the Beautiful

2. O beautiful for pilgrim feet,
   Whose stern impassioned stress
   A thoroughfare for freedom beat
   Across the wilderness.

   America! America!
   God mend thine every flaw.
   Confirm thy soul in self control,
   Thy liberty in law.

34 AMERICA

Words by Samuel Francis Smith

Henry Carey (?)
(c. 1689–1743)

35 OH, HOW LOVELY IS THE EVENING

German Round

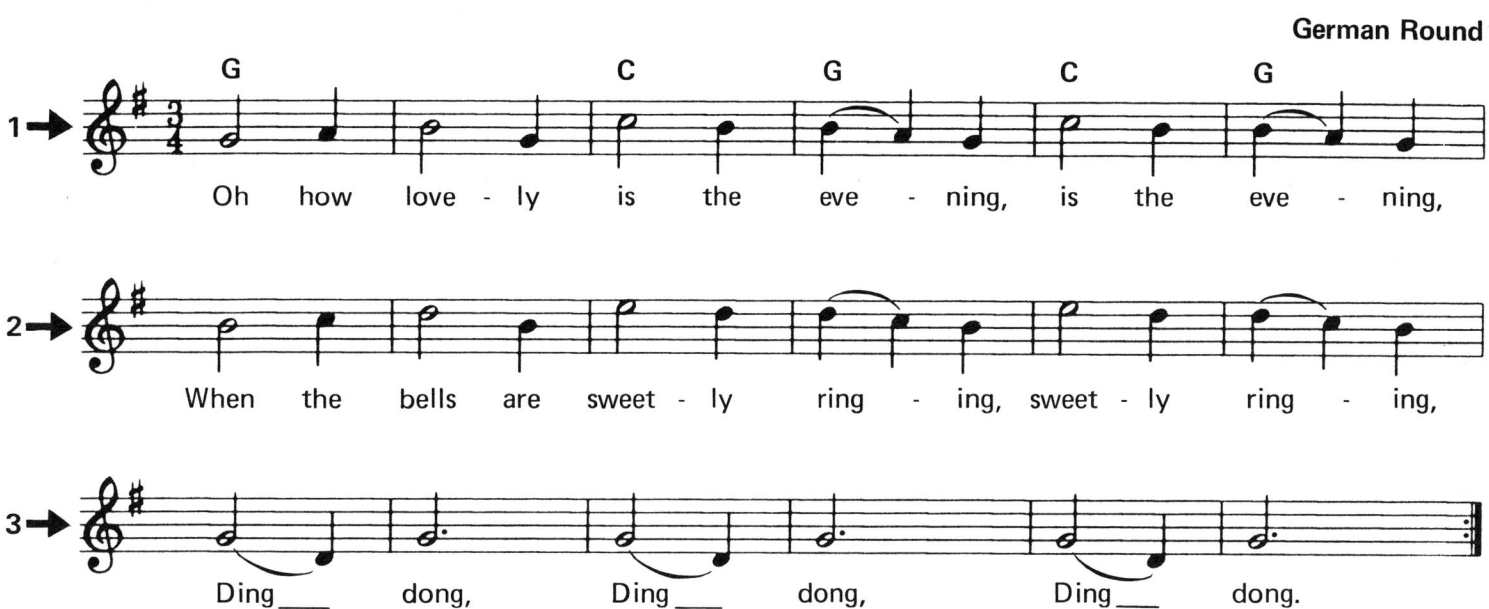

36 HEY, HO, NOBODY AT HOME

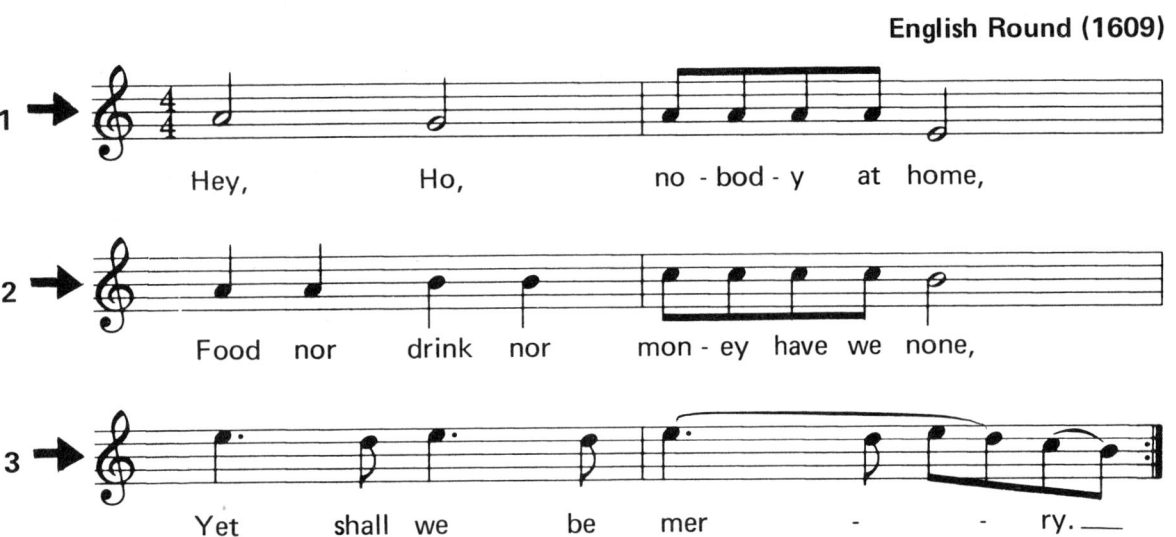

English Round (1609)

1. Hey, Ho, no-bod-y at home,
2. Food nor drink nor mon-ey have we none,
3. Yet shall we be mer - - ry.

37 DONA NOBIS PACEM

Traditional Round

38 SHALOM CHAVERIM

Israeli Round

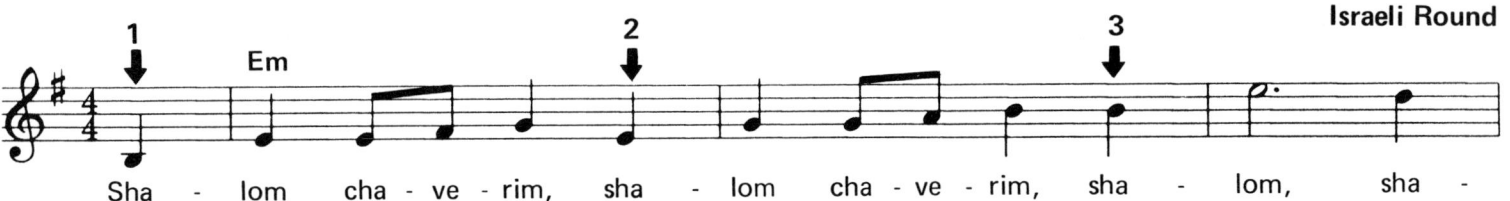

Sha - lom cha - ve - rim, sha - lom cha - ve - rim, sha - lom, sha -

lom, Le hit - ra - ot, le hit - ra - ot, sha - lom, sha - lom.

39 THE WELCOME SONG

18th-Century American Canon

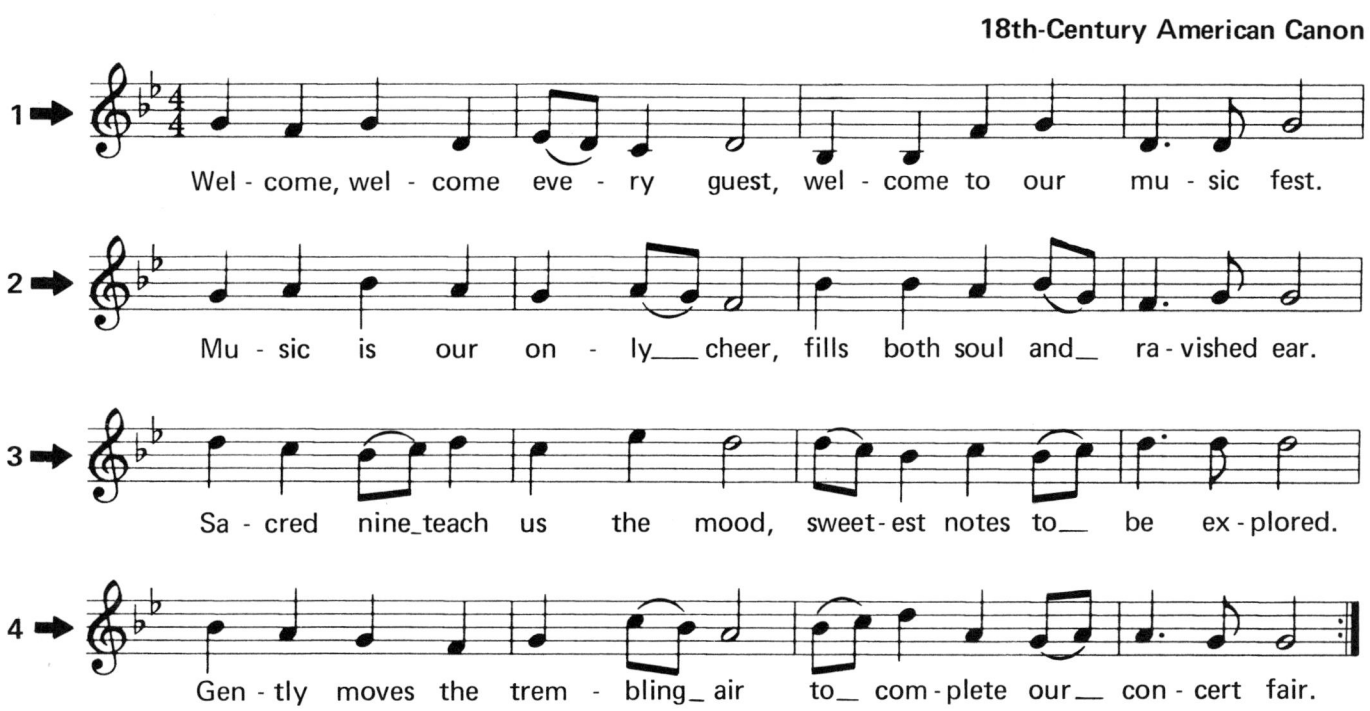

1. Wel - come, wel - come eve - ry guest, wel - come to our mu - sic fest.
2. Mu - sic is our on - ly cheer, fills both soul and ra - vished ear.
3. Sa - cred nine teach us the mood, sweet - est notes to be ex - plored.
4. Gen - tly moves the trem - bling air to com - plete our con - cert fair.

40 VICTIMAE PASCHALI

Gregorian Chant

Wipo
(c. 1000–1050)

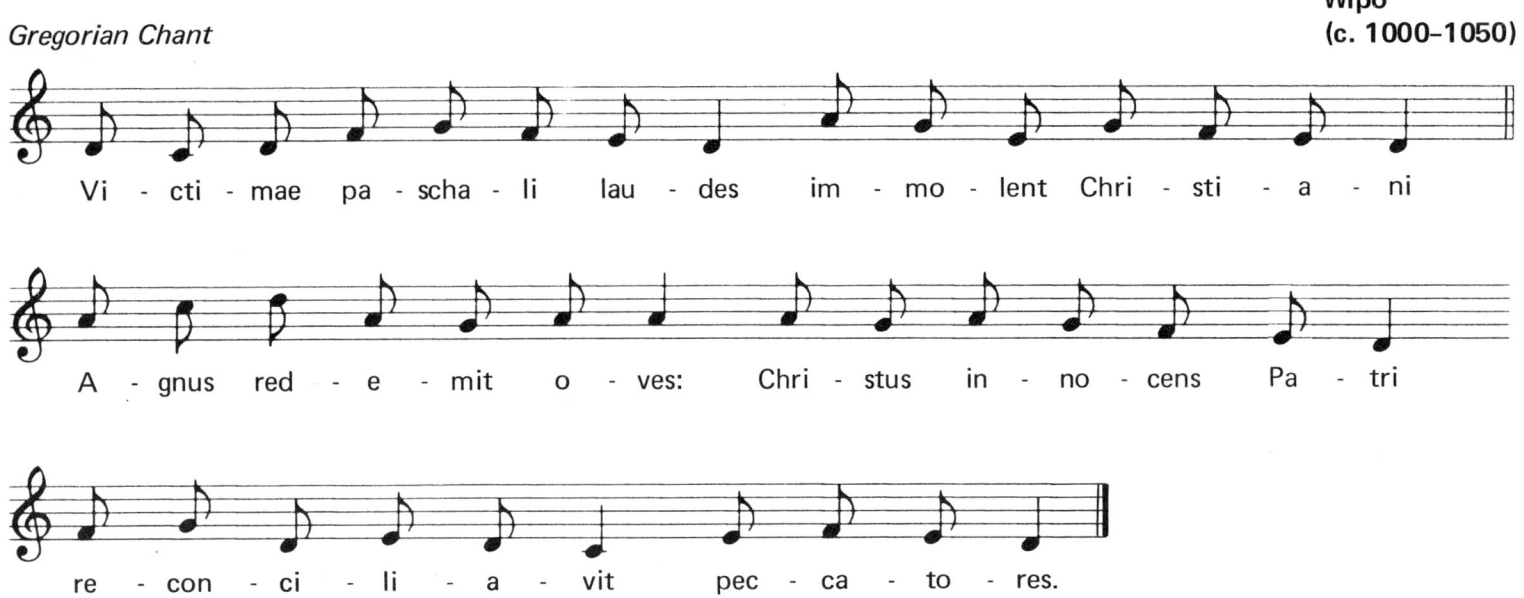

41 ADIEU, SWEET AMARILLIS

Four-part Madrigal for Mixed Voices

John Wilbye
(1574–1638)

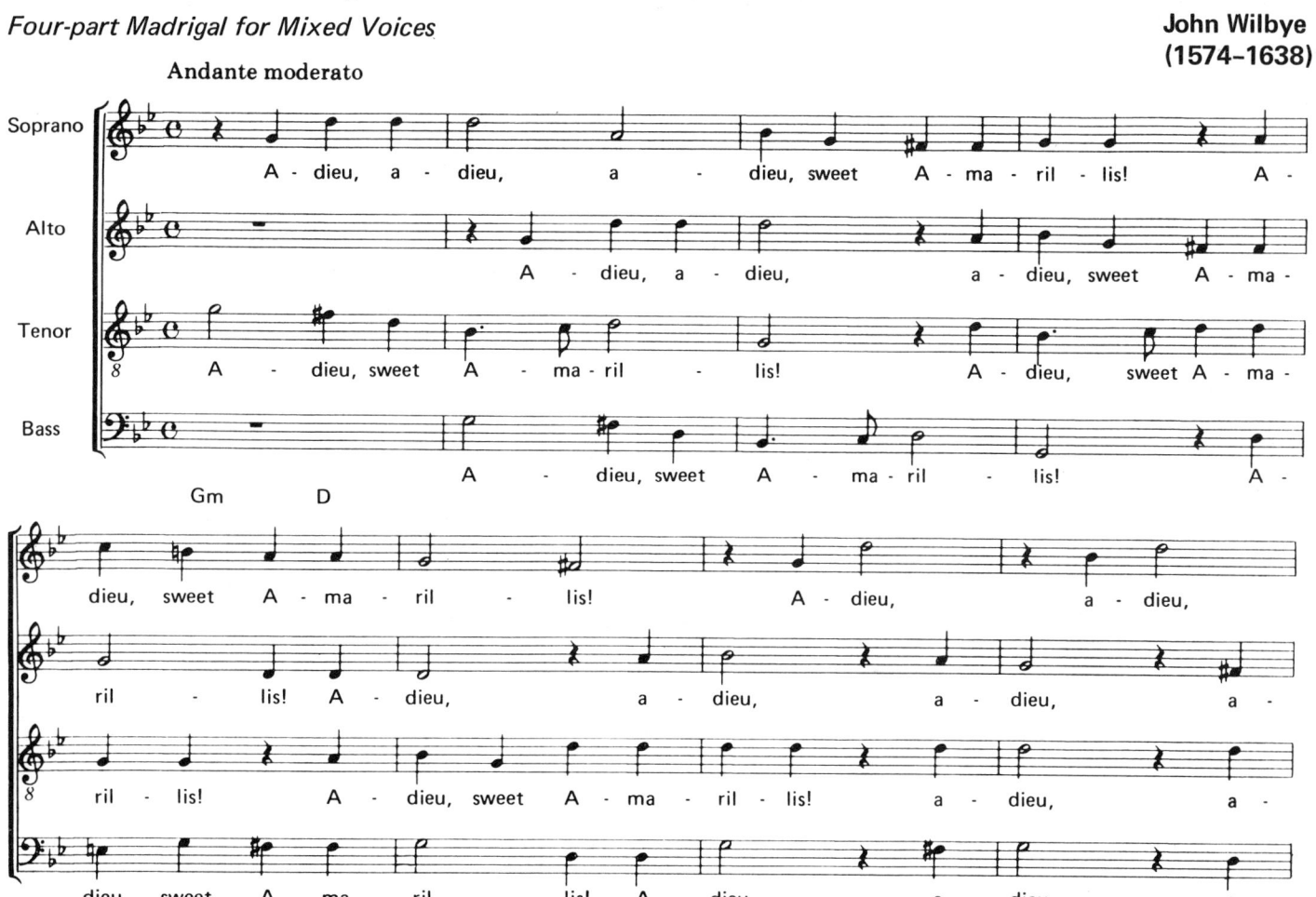

Adieu, Sweet Amarillis

Adieu, Sweet Amarillis

Adieu, Sweet Amarillis

Adieu, Sweet Amarillis

Adieu, Sweet Amarillis

42 THE YOUNG CONVERT

19th-Century New England Hymn

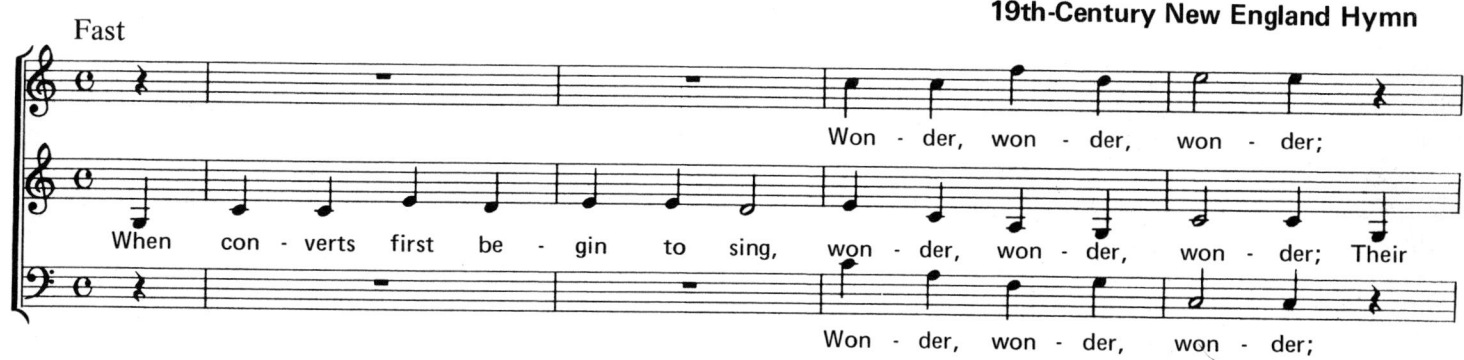
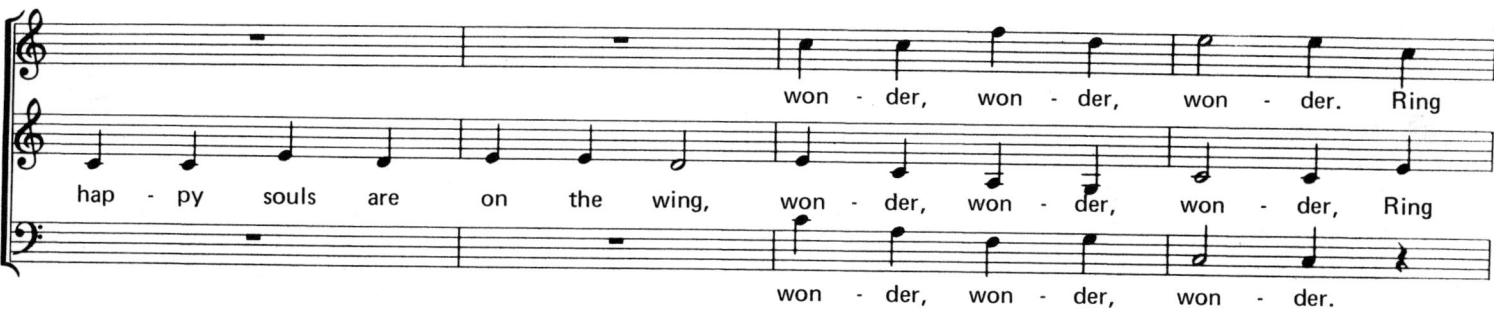

The Young Convert

43 WILLIE, TAKE YOUR LITTLE DRUM

Burgundian Carol
Arranged by L. Shelton

1. Willie, take your little drum, With your whistle Robin, come! When we hear the fife and drum, Turelurelu patapata pan, When we hear the fife and drum, Christmas should be frolicsome.

2. God and man are now become
   More than one with fife and drum.
   When you hear the fife and drum,
   Turelurelu, patapatapan,
   When you hear the fife and drum,
   Dance, and make the village hum!

44 REMEMBER, O THOU MAN

A Christmas Carol

Thomas Ravenscroft
(c. 1590-1663)

Remember, O Thou Man

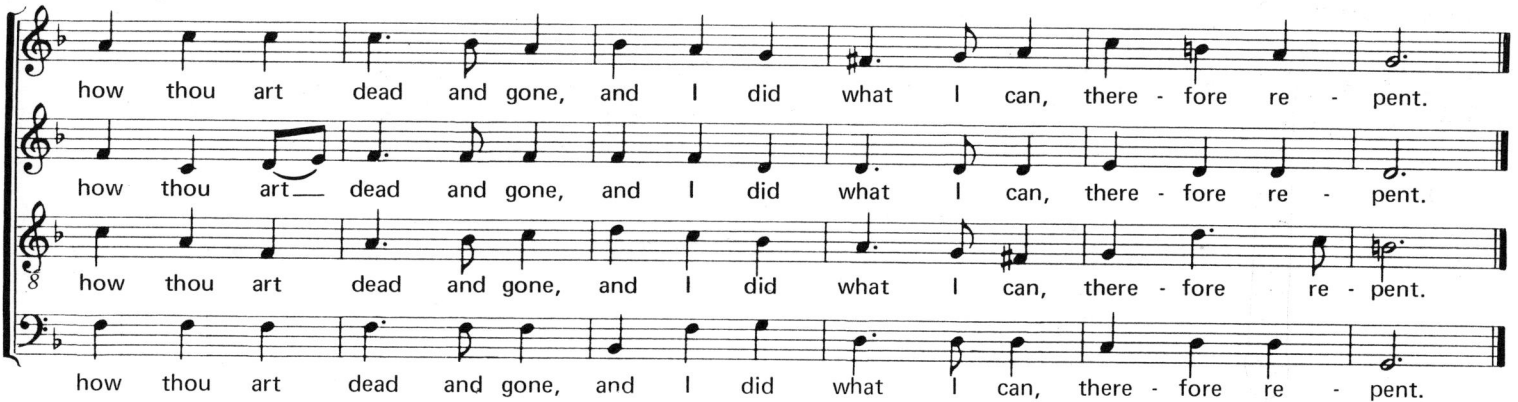

2. Remember God's goodnesse,
   O thou man, O thou man
   Remember God's goodnesse
   And his promise made.
   Remember God's goodnesse,
   How he sent his son doubtlesse
   Our sinnes for to redresse, be not affraid.

3. The Angels all did sing,
   O thou man, O thou man,
   The Angels all did sing
   Upon Shepheards hill.
   The Angels all did sing
   Praises to our heavenly King,
   And peace to man living with a good will.

45 SARABANDA

From Concerto Grosso, Opus 6, No. 11 (melody only)

Arcangelo Corelli
(1653–1713)

46 MINUET FOR LUTE

Robert Visée
(c. 1650–c. 1725)

Melody only

47 MINUET

Henry Purcell
(c. 1659–1695)

Melody only

48 MINUET K. 2

Wolfgang Amadeus Mozart
(1756-1791)

Minuet

58

49 STUDY IN C

For Guitar (excerpt)

Fernando Sor
(1778-1839)

50 ODE TO JOY

From Symphony No. 9 in D Major (melody only)

**Ludwig van Beethoven
(1770–1827)**

51 FUGUE IN C MINOR

From the Well-Tempered Clavier, Book I

Johann Sebastian Bach
(1685–1750)

Fugue in C Minor

Fugue in C Minor

52 WALTZ IN C-SHARP MINOR

Frédéric François Chopin
(1810–1849)

Opus 6, No. 2

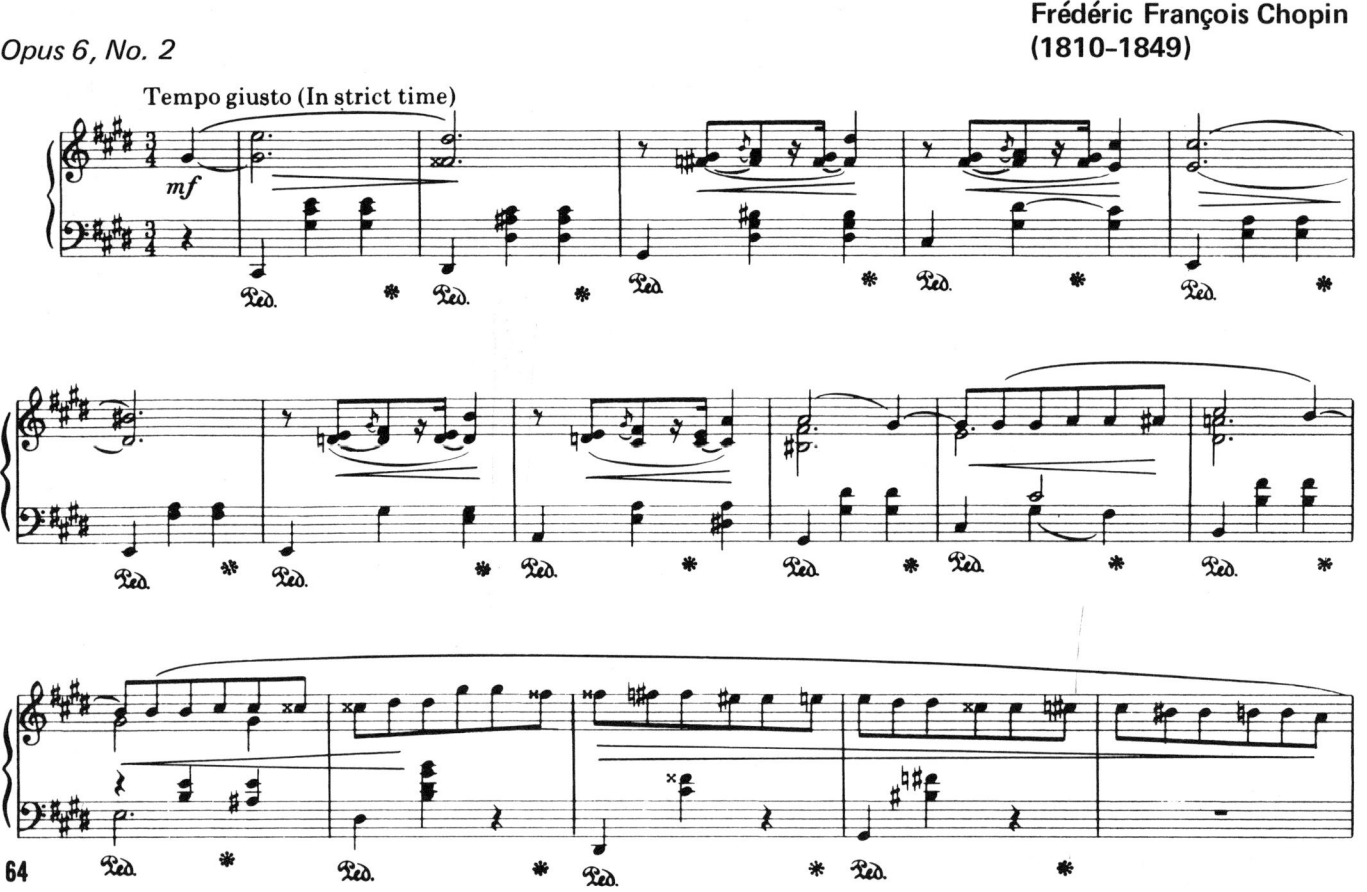

Waltz in C-Sharp Minor

Più mosso (A little faster)

Waltz in C-Sharp Minor

Waltz in C-Sharp Minor

Waltz in C-Sharp Minor

Waltz in C-Sharp Minor

Waltz in C-Sharp Minor

Waltz in C-Sharp Minor

Waltz in C-Sharp Minor

53 HOW STRANGE

Tom Manoff and Frank Feliciano

How Strange

How Strange